The Littl of Rhythm

by Judith Harries
Illustrations by Steve Evans

LITTLE BOOKS WITH **BIG** IDEAS

Published 2013 by Featherstone Education, an imprint of Bloomsbury Publishing Plc
50 Bedford Square, London, WC1B 3DP
www.bloomsbury.com

ISBN 978-1-4729-0256-6

Text © Judith Harries 2013
Illustrations © Steve Evans
Cover photographs © Shutterstock

Printed by Ashford Colour Press Ltd

1 3 5 7 9 10 8 6 4 2

This book is produced using paper that is made from wood grown in
managed, sustainable forests. It is natural, renewable and recyclable.
The logging and manufacturing process conform to the environmental
regulations of the country of origin.

To see our full range of titles visit
www.bloomsbury.com

Contents

Introduction

The aim of this Little Book is to provide practitioners with a rich and varied set of activities to introduce the basic musical concepts of beat and rhythm to young children in our early years settings.

Feeling the beat or 'pulse' in music is a basic instinctive response that most of us have when listening to or playing music. These songs, games and activities seek to recognise, encourage and develop our understanding of beat and rhythm. The performance raps or 'story poems' in the second half of the book are exciting opportunities for our children to explore and demonstrate their developing rhythmic skills.

Many of us shy away from singing and making music 'in front' of people – even the children in our care. Be assured that all of these activities can be managed and enjoyed by both non-specialist practitioners and music specialists alike. The secret is to use simple, well-known tunes and to play lots of games so that the learning is done as you go along.

Many of the rhythm activities and the raps can be used as part of different early years topics, and suggestions for these are included. There are also many opportunities for children to represent their own ideas, thoughts and feelings through their response to the activities.

Links with the EYFS framework

The prime areas of learning and development

Communication and language

▶ **Listening and attention**

Children listen to the raps and are encouraged to anticipate events and talk about characters within the story. There are many opportunities for dramatic interpretation. The children are often encouraged to listen to others and to be involved in their own performance concurrently.

▶ **Understanding**

Some activities require children to follow layers of instructions involving musical ideas. They can ask and answer 'how' or 'why' questions related to characters, settings and dramatic ideas.

▶ **Speaking**

These activities help children to express themselves effectively with a developing awareness of an audience. They can develop their own narratives and explanations by connecting ideas in stories.

Physical development

▶ **Moving and handling**

Many of the rhythm activities involve opportunities to show good control and coordination in large and small movements. They have to move around confidently with good spatial awareness. They learn to handle musical instruments effectively.

▶ **Health and self-care**

Children can demonstrate awareness of ways to keep healthy and safe alongside basic dressing skills when using dramatic costumes.

Personal, social and emotional development

▶ **Self-confidence and self-awareness**

Many of these activities require children to try out new challenges, singing and playing different instruments. They need to be confident to sing and speak in a group and talk about the different activities.

▶ **Managing feelings and behaviour**

Talking about different characters' feelings in the performance raps will help children to understand their own and other's behaviour. Many activities help the children to work as part of a group, following agreed rules and developing a good grasp of right and wrong.

▶ **Making relationships**

There are many opportunities in these rhythm activities to practise taking turns as children play circle games and work with 'talk partners'. They learn to consider and respect each other's ideas.

The specific areas of learning and development

Literacy

▶ **Reading**

Children are given opportunities to read their names and simple repeated sentences in choruses. They can demonstrate understanding when talking with others about what they have read.

▶ **Writing**

Some activities involve children using their phonic knowledge to write common words and use them in rhythm games.

Mathematics

▶ **Numbers**

Some rhythm activities include opportunities to count items and say which number is 'one more' or 'one less' than a given number.

▶ **Shape, space and measures**

Children will use everyday language to talk about recognising rhythm patterns and to identify repeated patterns. They can explore characteristics of everyday objects and shapes and use mathematical language to describe them.

Understanding of the world

▶ **People and communities**

They recognise similarities and differences between themselves and others, particularly in terms of likes and dislikes.

▶ **The world**

There are lots of opportunities to talk about changes and why some things occur. Many of the performance raps encourage children to talk about features of their own environment and similarities and differences between countries.

▶ **Technology**

They see a range of technology being used at home and school to listen to music.

Expressive arts and design

▶ **Exploring and using media and materials**

Many activities include songs and rhymes, and children can begin to build up a repertoire. They can explore the sounds of different instruments. They can experiment with ways of changing music by varying tempo (fast/slow) and dynamics (loud/quiet). There are opportunities to explore a variety of materials involved in musical instruments and in designing props and costumes for performance.

▶ **Being imaginative**

There are many opportunities in the performance raps to express feelings. Moving in response to music is at the very heart of many of the beat and rhythm activities. Creating their own rhythms is encouraged in activities like 'Clap in the gap' and 'Ostinato rhythms'. They are encouraged to represent their own ideas, thoughts and feelings through the performance raps.

How to use this book

The first five sections of this book move step-by-step through many aspects of the concepts of beat and rhythm in music. They begin by introducing the concept of a steady pulse or beat, then move on through activities exploring the duration or length of sounds, developing an understanding and experience of rhythm, combining and contrasting beat and rhythm, and a simple introduction to rhythm notation.

It is not necessary to work through each activity strictly in order, but the sequence of sections in this book has been carefully devised to create a developmental approach to learning about beat and rhythm. Try dipping into activities within each section but don't jump about too much!

Each beat and rhythm activity includes lists of 'What you need' and 'What you do', which outline the steps to take, followed by a further idea to extend the learning – 'Whatever next?'. Some of the song words in the activities include bold type to indicate where the beat of the song lies and to assist with teaching.

The second half of the book includes seventeen raps based on either traditional tales or popular early years topics. The raps can be enjoyed at any time and used in different ways, either as simple 'story poems' or as material to be performed in class assemblies, in front of the whole school and parents. There are 'Performance extras' included with each rap, which offer suggestions for how to teach the rap, considering solo, group and unison (all together) parts, ideas for props and costumes, and musical accompaniments where appropriate.

Keeping the beat

What you need:

▶ A selection of music with a strong beat (see 'Listening list', page 85).

What you do:

▶ Sit in a circle. Listen to some music with a strong beat or pulse and start tapping on your knees in time to the beat. Invite children to join in.

▶ Tap on different parts of the body such as shoulders, head, toes and nose. Stand up and tap your feet in time to the beat. Can the children copy you when you change the actions?

▶ Invite children to take turns being the leader for the others to follow.

▶ Try this chant to the beat and change the words appropriately:

Keep the beat,
With your [feet],
Keep the beat,
On the street.

▶ Try singing this traditional song and move different parts of the body in time to the beat. Add more parts of the body with each verse so the song grows longer.

Little Johnny dances, on my *thumb he dances,
Little Johnny dances, on my *thumb he dances,
*On my thumb, thumb, thumb,
Little Johnny dances.

v.2 *knee/On my knee, knee, knee.
v.3 *head/On my head, head, head.

Whatever next?
Repeat the beat games with some different recorded music at a faster or slower tempo (speed).

Moving to the beat

What you need:

▶ A selection of music with a strong beat (see 'Listening list', page 85).

▶ Suitable props to use such as brushes, brooms, scarves, etc.

What you do:

▶ Stand in a circle and listen to some music with a strong beat. Ask the children how it makes them feel. Do they naturally want to start moving or dancing?

▶ Start by tapping toes or feet in time to the beat.

▶ Ask the children to march like soldiers to the beat, swinging their arms and lifting their knees high.

▶ Provide a selection of props for them to use as they move to the beat.

▶ Ask children to wave the scarves back and forth as they step to the beat of the music.

▶ Try singing this song to the tune of 'What shall we do with the drunken sailor?'

Wave the scarves in the sky,
In the sky, in the sky,
Waves the scarves in the sky,
Watch them flying high.

▶ Invite children to use brushes or small brooms to sweep in time to the beat.

▶ Try chanting these words:

Sweeping brooms, across the floor,
This way, that way, and once more.

Whatever next?

Sit in a circle and ask children to hold onto a loop of elastic rope. When they are all holding on invite them to move the rope forwards and backwards in time to the beat as they chant these words together:

In and **out**, x 2

Up and **down**, x 2

Side to **side**, x 2

Here we **go again**.

Beanie 'beat bags'

What you need:

▶ Bean bags – coloured bean bags usually used as sports equipment, or soft toy versions such as Beanie Babies, should work as 'beat bags'. Make sure you have one for each child in the group.

What you do:

▶ Provide each child with a suitable bean bag that makes a sound when tapped onto another surface. Explain that you are going to use the bean bags to keep the beat.

▶ Ask them to join in this simple song to the tune of 'In and out the dusky bluebells':

Tap the **beat** as you **sing**, x 3

Tap to the **beat** like **me**.

▶ Start by holding the beat bag in one hand and tapping it on the other hand as you sing. Then try tapping other parts of the body such as knees, toes, head, etc. Can the children suggest some other actions to try?

▶ Try tapping the beat bags on the floor to make a louder tapping sound.

Whatever next?
Try to relate the 'beat bags' you use to topics in your setting; so Beanie Babies are great for work on Animals, Farms and Seasons, while normal bean bags are good for reinforcing colour recognition.

Heart beats

What you need:

▶ Hearts cut out of plastic or card, one for each child in the group.

▶ A selection of music with a strong beat (see 'Listening list', page 85).

What you do:

▶ Talk to children about how the heart pumps blood around the body as it beats. Explain that you can feel blood moving through the arteries when they are close to your skin. These are called pulse points.

▶ Help children to find these by placing three fingers to the side of the Adam's apple in their neck. Can they feel a regular up and down movement or pulse?

▶ Relate this regular pulse to the beat in music.

▶ Sit in a circle. Let children hold the plastic or cardboard hearts and move them in and out of the circle in time together. Can they do this in time to some music with a strong beat or pulse?

► Try singing this chant as they make the hearts move in time to the beat:

I can feel my heart beat, x 3

Sitting in my seat.

Add a strong drum beat so all children can hear the beat as they sing.

► Stand in a circle. Change the words of the chant. Divide the children into groups so some are beating, some are tapping and some are stamping.

I can **feel** my **heart beat**,

I can **feel** my **hand tap**,

I can **feel** my **feet stamp**,

Walking **down** the **street**.

Whatever next?

Ask the children what they think happens to their heartbeat during and after exercise. Test this out by feeling the pulse before and after some aerobic exercise. Explain that the pulse or beat in music sometimes speeds up or slows down too. Listen to some music that changes tempo (see 'Listening list', page 85).

Junk beats

What you need:

▶ Different pairs of items to tap together, such as plastic lids from polish spray or fabric softener bottles, small flower pots, yoghurt pots, pencils, plastic tubes, wooden bricks, etc.

What you do:

▶ Explain to the children that they can now play the beat using homemade or junk instruments.

▶ Start with pairs of plastic bottle tops (see above), matching colours and sizes. Show children how to hold the insides of the tops and tap the bottoms together.

▶ Try some 'tapping tops' songs and tap the beat as you sing:

[Tune: 'In and out']

Tap the **tops, as** you **sing**, x 3

Tap to the **beat** like **me**.

[Tune: 'London Bridge']

Tap the **tops**, just like **me**,

Just like **me**, just like **me**,

Tap the **tops**, just like **me**,

Tap the **tops** to**gether**.

▶ Now try with different junk pairs related to themes such as flower pots (Spring/gardens), yoghurt pots (food), pencils (work), bricks (colours/toys), etc.

▶ Can the children suggest any other items they could use to tap together to keep the beat?

Whatever next?

Organise the children in to groups of junk instruments and create a junk beat orchestra. Ask them to play along to your drum beat played on a biscuit tin, or saucepan with a wooden spoon of course!

Busy beat band

What you need:

▶ A selection of classroom instruments, one per child.

▶ A drum or cowbell.

What you do:

▶ Sit in a circle. Place an instrument in front of each child. Choose instruments that are good for keeping the beat such as claves, boomwhackers®, small drums, tambourines, bells, etc.

▶ Give children an opportunity to explore the sound of their instrument. Use simple hand signals such as 'opening hand, palm upwards' to start and 'closing fists' to stop.

▶ Stand in a circle and play a slow pulse or beat on a loud instrument such as a drum or cowbell.

▶ Invite the children to join in. It will often speed up, so if this happens stop the beat and ask the children what they think happened.

▶ Try again and ask children to try hard not to speed up, or slow down!

Whatever next?

Try singing this song to the tune of 'The wheels on the bus' as the children play their instruments:

We are **play**ing in the **busy** beat **band**,
The **busy** beat **band**, the busy beat **band**.
We are **play**ing in the **busy** beat **band**,
All day long.

Beat toys, make noise

What you need:

- ▶ Hard plastic cups, one for each child.
- ▶ Soft plastic toys that make a sound when tapped on the floor such as animals, vehicles, tools, balls, etc.

What you do:

- ▶ Ask children to copy you as you clap 4 times, 1, 2, 3, 4, and then repeat – keeping the steady count going with a slightly louder clap on the first beat.

- ▶ Show children how to tap with two fingers onto the palm of the other hand. This creates a quieter sound. Try this pattern – clap, tap, tap, tap.

- ▶ Now try placing the hard plastic cups upside down on the floor and tapping them as you count.

- ▶ Mix claps and cups – clap, clap, cup, cup – while still maintaining the steady count of the beat. Try tapping the other end of the cup for a new sound.

- ▶ Can the children invent some new patterns using the claps and cups?

> ### Whatever next?
> Explore sounds children can make by using soft plastic toys tapped on the floor in time to the beat as you sing.

The art of claves No. 1

What you need:

▶ Pairs of claves, enough for each child in the group. Sets of coloured claves are ideal for these activities. Alternatively, make your own using dowelling, cut and sanded so safe for small hands.

▶ A louder pair of claves for the practitioner!

What you do:

▶ Provide a pair of claves for each child. Place them on the floor in front of each child. On an agreed signal, ask the children to pick them up and hold them one in each hand, upright on their knees. This is called the 'silent place' because the claves cannot touch or make a noise.

▶ Show the children how to play the claves in different ways:

  ▷ Hold one clave still in a slightly cupped hand so there is space under the clave. Tap with the other clave.

  ▷ Hold one clave upright in a loose fist – like a nail. The other clave is used like a hammer to tap the nail.

  ▷ Hold the claves lengthways and tap together to make a loud sound.

  ▷ Tap the tips of the claves together to make a quieter sound.

▶ Compare and talk about the different effects these create. Which way of playing do the children prefer?

▶ Start playing a steady beat on the louder claves and invite the children to join in. Try adding the 1, 2, 3, 4 count.

Whatever next?

Introduce the 'clave wave' to tidy the claves away. Pass a basket or two around the circle and invite each child to play their claves once, before placing them in the basket and pushing it on to the next child. This method can also be reversed for giving out the claves.

Round-a-beat games

What you need:

▶ A loud drum or cowbell to keep the beat.
▶ A big ball.

What you do:

▶ Sit in a circle and start tapping a regular slow beat on the drum or cowbell. Invite children to join in clapping the beat. Remind them not to let the beat speed up.

▶ Explain that you are going to try and pass the beat around the circle.

▶ Ask the first child to clap once with the beat and then the next child in the circle does the same until the clap has passed all the way round.

▶ Some children may need you to walk around the circle with the drum as the clapped beat goes round, so that you can use eye contact or a movement of the drum to help them to know when it's their turn.

▶ When the group can do this, try passing round a pattern such as 'clap, tap' (tap knees) or even 'clap, tap, head' (tap knees then head).

▶ Now try passing a ball in time to the beat. Make sure the beat is slow and steady. Remind the children to listen to your drum beat. If they pass too fast, remind them that the objective of the game is to keep a steady pulse and that it's not a race!

Whatever next?

Can the children think of different actions to pass round the circle in time to the beat, such as a smile, nod of the head, stamp or dance move?

Passing games No. 1

What you need:

▶ An empty pie dish.
▶ A plastic or real apple.

What you do:

▶ Teach the children this simple song to the tune of 'Rain, rain, go away':

Me, my, me-oh, **my,**
How I **love** my **ap**ple **pie.**

▶ Invite the children to sit in a circle and tap the beat on their knees as they sing.
▶ Try passing an aluminium foil pie dish around the circle in time to the beat as they sing.
▶ Each time the song stops, whoever is holding the dish can choose which type of pie to sing about, for instance plum, blackberry, strawberry, chocolate, chicken, mushroom, etc. Or try some fantasy pies – eyeball, worm, buttercup, etc.!
▶ Try this passing game using a plastic or real apple and the same tune as before:

Apple tree, apple tree, will your apple fall on me?
I won't cry, and I won't shout, if your apple knocks me out!

▶ Pass an apple around the circle in time to the beat as they sing. Practise by walking round the circle, gently tapping two beats on each child's head using a laminated picture of an apple. Then repeat with one tap as they pass the apple. On the word 'out!', the child holding the apple is 'out' until the last one left in wins the apple!

Whatever next?

Change the passing game into a 'choosing game' to select children for different activities. Pass a toy or instrument such as a drum around the circle in time to the **beat** as you sing this song to the tune of 'Hot cross buns':

Who will **play, who** will **play**?
Pass the toy/drum **around** the ring and
It will **say!**

Section Two: Duration

These activities explore the duration (or length) of sounds, and how this creates rhythms.

Exploring long and short sounds

What you need:

▶ A selection of classroom instruments: some that make long sounds, some that make short sounds.

▶ A stop watch.

What you do:

▶ Talk about long and short sounds with the children. Listen to sounds around them and make a list. Can they hear any sounds that are short, like a cough, squeak or knock? Can they hear any sounds that last for a longer duration, such as a fan or computer whirring or an alarm ringing?

▶ Sing this song using long and short sounds to the tune of 'Frère Jacques':

Sing a **short** sound,   x2

Make it **long** _____,   x2

Can you hear the **short** sounds?

Can you hear the **long** sounds?

In this **song** _____.   X2

Can the children tell you which words sound the longest?

▶ Sit in a circle and place a different instrument in front of each child. Allow them time to experiment with the sounds the instruments can make. Use stop and start signals as before (see 'Busy beat band', page 16).

▶ Ask children to try and make short sounds on their instruments – one tap on a drum or clave, one shake of a maraca, a click of a castanet, etc.

▶ Then ask children to make some long sounds on some other instruments – one tap on a triangle, cowbell, chime bar or Indian bell, etc.

Whatever next?

Place two coloured hoops on the floor, labelled 'long' and 'short'. Which instruments are best at making short sounds? (Wooden and plastic instruments.) Which instruments are best at making long sounds? (Metal and skin instruments.) Help the children to sort the instruments into the appropriate sets. Are there any overlaps?

A sound experiment

What you need:

▶ Three or four instruments that make a long sound such as triangle, chime bar, Indian bells, cowbell, agogo bells, rain stick, etc.

▶ A stop watch.

What you do:

▶ Let the children recap what they remember about instruments making long and short sounds. Explain that you are going to organise an experiment to find out which instrument makes the longest sound.

▶ Help them to select three or four instruments to test. Ask children to predict which one will play the longest sound. Write down their predictions.

▶ Invite a child to play each instrument by tapping it once. Stand an equal distance away from each instrument and use a stopwatch to time how long the sound lasts for. Alternatively, count seconds slowly in your head and then children can join in too. Remember that children closer to the instrument may hear the sound for longer.

▶ Record the results on a simple chart:

Name of instrument	Length of sound in seconds

▶ Were the children surprised by the results? Were their predictions correct?

Whatever next?

Play some other musical instruments to the children such as piano, guitar, recorder and violin. Use live or recorded music to show them long and short sounds on these instruments.

Sounds around the ring

What you need:

▶ A selection of classroom instruments that make long and short sounds.

What you do:

▶ Explain to the children that patterns of long and short sounds create 'rhythms'.

▶ Sit in a circle and place alternate long and short sounding instruments in front of the children. Invite them to experiment with their instruments using the stop and start signals as before (see 'Exploring long and short sounds', page 24).

▶ Ask children to practise making a sound on their instrument by tapping, shaking or scraping it once.

▶ Now pass a sound around the ring so that each child has to play his or her sound. Listen to the alternate long and short sounds.

▶ Remind children not to make their sound until the sound before has stopped. Sometimes they will have a long wait, sometimes a very short one!

Whatever next?

Create long and short sounds in layers or textures. Ask all the children who can make long sounds to play their instruments together very quietly. Every time their sound stops, invite them to play again. Listen to the sustained texture of sounds this creates. Invite children who can make short sounds to interrupt the texture with their sudden sounds. How does this music make the children feel?

Long and short patterns

What you need:

▶ A selection of classroom instruments that make long and short sounds.

▶ Thin strips of cardboard, and felt pens.

What you do:

▶ Remind the children that patterns of long and short sounds create rhythms.

▶ Scribe some long and short marks on the white board, for example:

— — · ·

What do the children think these marks mean? Invite two volunteers to demonstrate and read the symbols.

▶ Sit in a circle and place alternate long and short sounding instruments in front of the children. Ask all the 'long sounds' to play together and then all the 'short sounds'.

▶ Sort the children into pairs around the circle so there is a long and short sound in each pair.

▶ Provide each pair with a long strip of cardboard and two coloured felt pens. Ask them to scribe a pattern of long sounds (dashes) and short sounds (dots). Ask them to limit the total number of marks to four to start with.

▶ Invite the children to practise playing the pattern they have written down with their partner. Can they perform it to the rest of the children?

▶ Film the children playing their long and short patterns.

Whatever next?

Choose a particularly successful pattern and ask the pair of children to play it over and over again. Explain to the children that this repeated pattern or rhythm is called an 'ostinato'. Listen to some music with a strong ostinato or riff (see 'Listening list', page 85).

Section Three: Rhythm games

Lots of activities and games to develop understanding and experience of rhythm.

Echo clapping

What you need:

▶ Lots of simple rhythm patterns in your head! The more you practise, the easier this becomes.

What you do:

▶ Stand in a circle and ask children to copy whatever you do, as in a follow-the-leader game. Try some simple actions such as waving, clapping, stamping, clicking, tapping shoulders, etc.

▶ Sit down in a circle. Explain that you want the children to listen and copy or echo whatever you clap. If they begin to clap at the same time as you, try saying 'my turn, your turn' to remind them when to respond.

▶ Start with just four claps while counting **1**, 2, 3, 4 in a steady beat. Hold your hands open with the palms upwards as a sign for them to echo your claps.

▶ When the children can copy this accurately try some simple rhythms such as:

     _ _ .. _ (long, long, short short, long)

     .. .. _ _ (short, short, long, long)

     _ .. _ _ (long, short, short, long, long)

▶ Ask the children to try and start their echo as soon as your pattern is done. If possible, demonstrate with another adult or a child who has grasped the idea quickly.

▶ Introduce some different dynamics (loud and quiet) by clapping for loud and tapping with two fingers for quiet.

> ## Whatever next?
> When the children are more confident, invite them to take turns being the leader and clapping a pattern for the other children to echo.

Rhythm whispers

What you need:

▶ Previous experience of echo clapping!

What you do:

▶ Sit in a circle and play a game of 'Chinese whispers'. Remind the children that the message should stay the same as it passes round the circle.

▶ Explain that you are going to try and pass a rhythm around the circle – 'rhythm whispers' – and try not to change it as it goes round.

▶ Emphasise that the children must echo clap exactly what their neighbour claps to them. This is a good way of assessing how well the children can echo a rhythm pattern.

▶ Start with a simple four beat clap and then repeat with some more interesting patterns such as __ . . __ . . / . __ . __ __

▶ Incorporate some other body percussion ideas such as stamp, clap clap, stamp, click.

▶ Invite children to make up a 'rhythm whisper' to pass round.

▶ If the pattern changes, can some of the children identify where the pattern was changed? – with no blame attached, of course!

Whatever next?

Provide a pair of claves for each child and invite a volunteer to play a rhythm pattern on the claves to pass round the circle. Does the pattern stay unaltered all the way around? Repeat with different classroom instruments and concentrate on the rhythm pattern and not the timbre (sound) of the instrument.

Clap in the gap

What you need:

▶ Previous experience of echo clapping!

What you do:

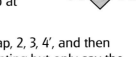

▶ Sit in a circle and warm up with some echo clapping.

▶ Explain to the children that they are going to have a go at inventing or making up their own rhythm patterns.

▶ Ask them to join in with you as you clap and count 'Clap, 2, 3, 4', and then 'Stop, 2, 3, 4'. Then ask them to keep clapping and counting but only say the numbers in their heads using the 'thinking voice'.

▶ Repeat this over and over again until a pattern is established of four claps and four counts of silence, so creating 'gaps'.

▶ Demonstrate how to 'clap in the gap' by just clapping four times on your own. Invite individual children to have a go on their own.

▶ Then demonstrate clapping a rhythm pattern in the gap such as __ __ . . __

▶ Choose four children to have a go at clapping any rhythm pattern in the gap. Always leave the first gap empty to remind them how long they need to clap. If they cannot think of anything to clap, tell them to just clap four times and it will fit!

▶ Eventually you can try going round the circle with every child taking a turn at playing clap in the gap. Try to get all the way round without someone going 'shy' or not being ready – that is a great achievement!

Whatever next?

Can the children think of other ways they could play rhythms in the gap, i.e. using body percussion such as stamps, clicks, taps, nods, etc.? Progress onto playing different classroom instruments in the gap.

▶ Alternatively, pass a soft toy or bean bag around the ring as you sing this song to the tune of 'Knees up, Mother Brown':

Come and **play** the **drum**, x2

Come and **play** a clever **rhy**thm,

Rum tum, **tum** tum **tum**.

▶ Whoever is holding the bean bag at the end has to play a rhythm on the drum for the others to echo clap.

Whatever next?

Provide a selection of classroom instruments including claves, drums, tambourines, maracas and castanets, one per child. Ask the children to copy the drum rhythms on their instruments.

Passing games No.3

What you need:

▶ Soft toy or puppets of a cat and mouse.

▶ Two contrasting stars, big/small or hard/soft.

▶ Two small drums or djembes.

What you do:

▶ Sit in a circle around the drums. Play a game of 'Cat and mouse catch'.

▶ Position the cat and mouse toys in two different starting places around the circle. Ask the children to pass them round as quickly as they can.

▶ The cat has to try and catch up with the mouse as they chase around the circle.

▶ When the cat has caught the mouse, the child holding both toys can go into the middle of the circle to play one of the drums and chooses a friend to play the other.

▶ Can they play some rhythm patterns on the drums for each other to echo?

▶ Show the children the two contrasting stars. I use a real dried starfish that rattles quietly when shaken and a large soft star with a very loud squeaker inside. Talk about the different loud/quiet sounds.

▶ Pass the two stars around the circle in opposite directions as you sing this song to the tune of 'Rain, rain , go away':

Star light, star bright,
First star I see tonight,
Wish I may, wish I might,
Have the wish I wish tonight.

▶ Whoever gets the 'loud' star has to clap a loud rhythm pattern and the rest of the children echo clap back. The 'quiet' star holder has to tap a rhythm using two fingers for the other children to tap quietly back.

Whatever next?

Can the children invent a new passing game? Ask them to work with a partner and share their ideas. Remind them that they can pass an instrument, a sound or a toy.

Section Four: Beat and rhythm activities

These songs and activities combine and contrast beat and rhythm to develop understanding of both concepts.

Cobbler, cobbler, mend my shoe

What you need:

▶ A pair of claves for each child.

▶ A spare shoe.

I will need

What you do:

▶ Learn this version of the traditional song 'Cobbler, cobbler, mend my shoe':

Cobbler, **cob**bler, **mend** my **shoe**,

Get it **done** by **half** past **two**,

'**Cos** my **toe** is **peep**ing **through**,

Cobbler, **cob**bler, **mend** my **shoe**.

▶ Ask the children to tap the beat of the song on their knees as they sing.

▶ Pass out the claves using a 'clave wave' (see 'The art of claves No.1', page 19).

▶ Ask children to tap beat on the claves and then to take one clave and tap their shoes in time to the beat. Try tapping the floor with the other clave.

▶ Can they tap the beat alternating between shoe and floor?

▶ Explain that you are now going to explore the rhythm of the song. Change the last line to say: **Now** the **rhy**thm **starts** with **you**.

▶ Pass a shoe around the circle in time to the beat as they sing the song. Whoever is holding the shoe at the end of the song has to tap a rhythm on the floor with the shoe for all the children to copy.

▶ Ask the children to join in as you clap the rhythm of the words of each line. Do they notice anything about the rhythm? Each line has the same rhythm:

· · · · · · ▁

▶ Invite children to clap the rhythm of the words as they sing the song. Then try tapping the rhythm with the claves. How does it feel compared to tapping the beat? (Faster, busier, easier?)

▶ When the children are confident with the rhythm, divide them into two groups – one to tap the beat on their knees, one to clap the rhythm. Can both groups keep going all the way through the song?

▶ Now try using two groups of claves – one to play the beat and the other to play the rhythm!

Whatever next?

Try this process of learning a song, tapping the beat and then clapping the rhythm with other songs about shoes such as 'Diddle diddle dumpling', 'Cock-a-doodle-doo', 'One, two, buckle my shoe', and 'There was an old woman who lived in a shoe'.

Number songs

What you need:

▶ A pair of claves for each child.

What you do:

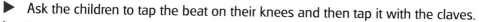

▶ Learn a number song such as:
Two, **four**, **six**, **eight**,
Meet me **at** the **ga**rden **gate**,
If I'm late, don't wait,
Two, **four**, **six**, **eigh**t.
[Tune: 'Rain, rain, go away']

▶ Ask the children to tap the beat on their knees and then tap it with the claves.

▶ Now clap the rhythm of the words as they sing them. Which two lines have the same rhythm pattern? (1 and 4.)

▶ Can the children notice anything else special about the rhythm of lines 1 and 4? (It's the same as the beat!)

▶ Introduce the idea of using the 'thinking voice', i.e. singing or thinking the words in your head. Can the children tap the beat and use their thinking voice for the words? Now try clapping the rhythm of the words and using the thinking voice. Does everyone finish clapping at the same time?

▶ Try clapping the rhythm of the words, and use the thinking voice for all the words except for the last word of each line, which is sung out loud. All you should hear is clapping and the words 'eight', 'gate', 'wait', and 'eight', all sung together!

▶ Divide the children into two groups and help one to tap the beat and one to clap the rhythm of the words.

Whatever next?

Can the children think of any other number rhymes or songs? Try 'This old man', 'One, two, buckle my shoe', 'Once I caught a fish alive' and 'Engine, engine, No.9'. Try some similar activities with these songs – singing, tapping the beat and clapping the rhythm of the words, using thinking voice, etc.

Pease pudding hot

What you need:

► A pair of claves for each child.

What you do:

► Learn the traditional song 'Pease pudding hot':

Pease pudding **hot**,

Pease pudding **cold**,

Pease pudding in the **pot**

Nine days old.

► This is a good song for introducing silences into rhythm patterns. Ask the children to tap the beat on their knees as they sing the song. Do they notice anything about the ends of lines 1, 2, and 4? There is a gap, silence or 'rest' with no words.

► Add a 'sh' sound and put fingers on lips at the ends of lines 1, 2, and 4 to mark the silence and explain that this is a break or rest in the rhythm.

► Now try clapping the rhythm of the words and mark the rest by moving the hands apart with palms upwards.

► Use the 'clave wave' to give out the claves and ask the children to put them in the 'silent place' on their knees. Use the claves to tap the rhythm of the words as they sing and put the claves in the silent place at the end of lines 1, 2, and 4 to mark the silence.

Whatever next?

Add silent actions to mark each of the rests: hot – blow out through pursed lips and wave one hand in front of face to indicate heat; cold – mime a shiver; old – hold the nose as though it smells horrid!

Ostinato rhythms

What you need:

▶ A selection of untuned classroom instruments.

What you do:

▶ Sit in a circle and try some echo clapping.

▶ Keep repeating the same rhythm pattern for the children to copy. After about 5 repeats, stop and see if anyone has noticed what has happened.

▶ Explain that sometimes you get 'stuck' when leading the echo clapping. Play 'Stuck in the groove'. As before, start with normal echo clapping, then repeat one pattern over and over. When the children notice, ask them to put their hands on their head and stop echoing.

▶ Introduce the concept of the repeated rhythm pattern as an 'ostinato'.

▶ Make up some clapping ostinatos (repeated patterns) for the children to join in with such as   .. __ .. __ (repeat) or . __ . __ sh (repeat).

▶ Try inventing some ostinatos using other body percussion such as 'stamp, clap clap, stamp, sh' (repeat).

▶ Provide an instrument for each child. Use the stop and start signals (see 'Busy beat band', page 16), so children can explore the sound of their instrument.

▶ Invite them to take turns to play a rhythm on their instrument for the other children to copy and repeat like an ostinato.

Whatever next?
Choose a simple rhythm pattern such as __ __ .. __ and all play it together as an ostinato. Try playing it as you sing together the nursery rhyme 'Polly put the kettle on'.

Hickory dickory dock

What you need:

▶ A pair of claves or a woodblock for each child.

What you do:

▶ Learn the song 'Hickory dickory dock':

Hickory dickory dock,

The mouse ran up the clock.

The clock struck one, the mouse ran down,

Hickory dickory dock.

▶ Ask children to tap on their knees to the beat as they sing the song. Then try adding the words 'tick tock' as they tap.

▶ Ask one group of children to sing and tap 'tick tock' as an ostinato (repeated pattern), while the other children sing the rhyme. Can they keep the clock ticking?

▶ Give out the claves and wood blocks to the ostinato group and use them to tap the 'tick tock' ostinato.

▶ Is there another rhythm in the song that could be used as an ostinato? Try using the phrase 'the clock struck one' and keep it going while the children sing the song.

▶ Ask a group of confident children to try and keep this new ostinato going using the wooden instruments.

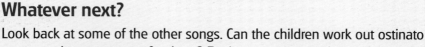

Whatever next?

Look back at some of the other songs. Can the children work out ostinato accompaniment patterns for them? For instance, try tapping and singing 'Half past two' as an ostinato while singing 'Cobbler, cobbler'.

44

Section Five: Rhythm notation

These games introduce simple rhythm notation or writing using pictures, words and musical symbols.

Picture patterns

What you need:

▶ Multiple pictures of a simple hand and foot, plus blu tack.

▶ A white board and pens.

▶ Selection of wooden, metal and skin instruments.

▶ Thin strips of cardboard and felt pens.

What you do:

▶ After lots of games, songs and activities using rhythm, children are ready to be introduced to simple graphic notation or music writing ideas.

▶ Start with pictures or symbols representing hands clapping and feet stamping.

▶ Draw a grid on the white board with four boxes. Stick on four pictures of hands. What do the children think this might mean? (Clap four times.)

▶ Change it to four pictures of feet. Can a volunteer work out what it means now? (Stamp four times.)

▶ Mix and match the pictures, for instance 3 hands + 1 foot = 3 claps + one stamp.

▶ Let the children come up to the board and mix up the pictures to create new body rhythm patterns for the other children to perform.

▶ Can they think of any other picture symbols to use for different body percussion sounds?

Whatever next?

Use simple symbols to represent instruments so children can notate patterns. For instance, x = wooden instruments, ▲ = metal instruments, o = skin instruments. Ask children to work with a partner to create a rhythm pattern to play on two instruments, e.g. o o x x

Name rhythms

What you need:

▶ A selection of classroom instruments.

▶ Cards with the children's names on.

What you do:

▶ Sing the song 'My name it has a rhythm', to the tune of 'My hat it has three corners':
My **name** it **has** a **rhy**thm,
A **rhy**thm I can **clap/tap**,
My **name** it **has** a **rhy**thm,
So listen **to** this **rap**.

▶ Pass a tambourine around the ring as the children sing the song. Whoever is holding the instrument at the end of the song can chant their name and then clap or tap the rhythm, for instance: Benjamin = . . . , Sophie = . . , Arek = . . , Grace = __ , Tyrese = . __ , etc.

▶ When everyone has got the idea, they should try saying and clapping their names one after the other around the circle, like a rap. Can they say their name and clap the rhythm at the same time?

▶ Give out instruments to all the children. Remind them not to play them until you give the 'start' sign.

▶ Invite them to have a go at playing their names on their instruments, all together. It will be quite noisy!

▶ Ask the children to go round the circle taking it in turns to say and play their name. It often requires a lot of restraint to only play one tap or shake on an instrument if your name is Jake!

Whatever next?

Put some name cards on the board. Who can read their own name? Ask for volunteers to read and clap their name. Add surnames and introduce instruments into the game!

Word rhythms

What you need:

▶ Pictures of different words to go with a variety of topics.

▶ Small cards, scissors, glue, etc.

What you do:

▶ Explain that all words have a rhythm when we say them. Choose two words to go with your current topic, one with one syllable and one with two syllables, for instance: the words for the topic 'colours' could be 'red' and 'yellow'; 'fruit' could be 'plum' and 'apple'; 'transport' could be 'car' and 'lorry', etc.

▶ Find pictures of the two words and make a small card for each, with the word and picture displayed. Stick four 'red' cards on the board in a grid. Can the children say the word 'red' four times in time to a steady beat: __ __ __ __?

▶ Ask the children to clap once each time they say the word 'red'.

▶ Show them the yellow cards. Stick four 'yellow' cards on the board in a grid. Can they say the word 'yellow' four times in time to a steady beat? . . . .
 . . . .
How many times will they clap for each 'yellow'? (Two times.)

▶ Make a sequence using the words, for instance: 'red, yellow, red, yellow'. Can the children say and clap the pattern: __ . . __ . . ?

▶ Let the children come up and make new patterns using the 'red' and 'yellow' cards for the group to say and clap.

Whatever next?

Suggest other early years topics and ask children to help you think of one and two syllable words for them. Examples could include: Animals – cat, giraffe; Garden – tree, flower, etc. Ask children to draw their own pictures for the notation cards.

Meet Sam and Susie

What you need:

▶ Two hand puppets.

▶ Musical notation (rhythm writing) cards showing crotchet and 2 quavers: ♩, ♫

I will need

What you do:

▶ Choose two hand puppets to introduce the musical symbols. I use a pirate puppet called Pirate Captain Samuel McTavistock, or 'Sam' for short! Make up your own backstory to introduce your puppets. 'Sam' uses the crotchet notation card as his musical name. Every time the children see him they say his name 'Sam' and clap once at the same time.

▶ Then introduce his friend the parrot who is called Susie. She uses the quavers notation card as her musical name and requires two claps.

▶ Make the puppets pop out from behind your back and see if the children can say and clap the right name.

▶ What happens if both puppets pop out together?

▶ Try Sam's 'Beat'. Use four 'crotchet' notation cards to make a beat for Sam. Can the children say and clap Sam's name four times?

▶ Try Susie's 'Groove'. Use four 'quavers' notation cards to create a pattern for Susie. Can the children say and clap Susie's name four times?

▶ Mix and match the cards and stick four on the whiteboard to notate rhythm patterns for the children to say and clap, for instance:

'Susie Sam Susie Sam', or 'Susie Susie Susie Sam'.

Whatever next?

Play 'All together now'. Place the notation cards face down on the floor and choose four children to pick one each. Stick them on the board and invite children to all read, say and clap the rhythm pattern together after a count of '1, 2, 3, 4.'

Rhythm bubbles

What you need:

- ▶ A whiteboard, pens and rubber.
- ▶ Previous experience of silences or 'rests' (see 'Pease pudding hot', page 42).

What you do:

- ▶ Sing 'Pease pudding hot' and remind children about silences and 'rests' in songs and rhythm patterns.

- ▶ Play a game of 'Rhythm bubbles'. Draw eight circles on the board in two rows of four. Write 'Sam' or a crotchet note in each circle on the top line, and 'Susie or quaver notes in each circle on the second line.

- ▶ Ask children to say and clap the rhythm pattern.

- ▶ Invite child to come up and rub out or 'pop' one bubble. Can they do it carefully so the sign inside is rubbed out but the circle or bubble remains?

- ▶ Now say and clap the pattern again and ask the children to leave a silence or rest for the empty bubble.

- ▶ Repeat until all the bubbles are 'popped'!

- ▶ Introduce the musical symbol for a rest or silence: 𝄽. It looks rather like a squiggle or wiggle on the page, so ask the children to wiggle their fingers each time they see this symbol. Ask them not to make a sound with their voices so they create a 'silence'.

- ▶ Repeat the 'rhythm bubbles' game but this time when each bubble is popped draw a wiggle or 'rest' in the space.

> ### Whatever next?
> Use the musical notation (rhythm writing) cards for 'Sam' and 'Susie', and add a wiggle or rest card. Play 'All together now' again (see 'Meet Sam and Susie', page 50). Remind children to wiggle their fingers when they read the rest card.

Notation games

What you need:

▶ Musical notation (rhythm) cards, showing ♩ , ♫ and 𝄽 (see Resources, page 87).

▶ Cut-out cardboard star shapes.

▶ Cardboard train and carriages.

What you do:

▶ Try a variety of different rhythm notation/writing games, using shapes related to an early year's theme such as 'Night and day' or 'Journeys'.

▶ Play 'Starry night'. Cut out lots of stars from shiny silver and gold card. Draw the musical notes onto the stars or else stick the notation cards onto them.

▶ Place the stars face down in the middle of the circle and choose four children to pick up a star and read the rhythm.

▶ Stick four stars onto the board and ask the children to say the rhythms together and then clap the rhythm pattern.

▶ The game 'Train rhythms' follows a similar pattern. Cut out a train engine and four carriages from cardboard and stick them onto the board.

▶ Ask the children to sit in a circle. Place the musical notation (rhythm) cards face-down in the middle of the circle and choose four children to pick up a card and stick it 'into' or on a train truck.

▶ Ask the children to say and clap the rhythms together. Can they repeat the pattern over and over like an ostinato (repeated pattern) so it creates the sound of the train?

▶ Introduce dynamics (loud/quiet) and ask children to clap or tap the rhythms. Can they clap the rhythms and use their 'thinking voice' for the rhythm names?

▶ Provide claves so the children can play the rhythms on instruments.

Whatever next?

Make up some new games using rhythm notation to relate to other early years themes, for instance: Food – cardboard apples on a tree with musical notation (music notes) written on one side; Autumn – coloured leaves on a tree, etc.

Fishing for rhythms

What you need:

▶ Card or plastic fish shapes, paper clips, and fishing rod with magnet.

What you do:

▶ Play 'Fishing for rhythms'. Draw the musical notation symbols (music notes) onto the plastic or card fish shapes. Add a paper clip to each fish shape and place them face down in the middle of a circle of children.

▶ Invite the children to take turns fishing for rhythms using a magnetic fishing rod. Stick four fish onto the board and ask the children to say the rhythm names using 'Sam', 'Susie' and 'wiggle'.

▶ Then all say and clap the rhythms together.

▶ Add two 'sharks' to the game with the words 'loud' and 'quiet' written on them. Ask the children to clap the rhythm pattern using loud claps or quiet taps.

▶ Add three 'starfish' to the game with the words 'wood', 'metal' and 'skin' written on them. Ask the children to play the rhythm pattern on an instrument from each family.

▶ Invite individual children to clap a four-beat 'fishing' rhythm on their own as a great way to assess their understanding of reading notation.

> ### Whatever next?
> When you have two or more four-beat fishing rhythms on the board, try a game of 'Rhythm quest'. Ask a volunteer to clap one of the rhythm patterns and see if the children can listen carefully and identify which rhythm they hear.

Section Six: Performance raps based on traditional tales

Three Billy Goats Gruff

Three Billy Goats Gruff were feeling rough,
The grass in their field was not fresh enough.
"We must go to the meadow, come on my fine fellows,"
Said the Billy Goats Gruff.

"Let's eat our share of the grass over there,
That's over the bridge with the troll in his lair.
He shouts and he roars, but you'd best ignore,"
Said the Billy Goats Gruff.

So Little Billy Goat fluffed up his coat
And stepped out so bravely, please take note.
Trotted over the rise, and closed his eyes,
As the troll woke up and then he cries:

"Who's that walking, not even talking,
Trip trap a-tripping over my bridge?"
"It's only me," says the goat, with a lump in his throat,
"But my big brother's coming, just you wait and see!"

So Middle Billy Goat fluffed up his coat
And stepped out so bravely, please take note.
Trotted over the rise, and closed his eyes,
As the troll woke up and then he cries:

"Who's that walking, not even talking,
Trip trap a-trapping over my bridge?"
"It's only me," says the goat, with a lump in his throat,
"But my big brother's coming, just you wait and see!"

So Big Billy Goat spiked up his coat
And stepped out so boldly, please take note.
Trotted over the rise, and opened his eyes,
As the troll woke up and then he cries:

"Who's that walking, not even talking,
Thump thump a-thumping over my bridge?"
"It's me," growled the goat, with a frog in his throat,
And I'm coming to get you, just you wait and see!"

Performance extras

▶ Read through the complete rap and talk about the different characters.

▶ Add taps, claps or stamps to the beat of the rap.

▶ Choose three children to play the parts of the Billy Goats.

▶ Talk about the different-sized goats using different voices. Can the Little Billy Goat use a quiet, high voice, the Middle Billy Goat a louder, normal voice, and the Big Billy Goat a loud, low voice?

▶ Experiment with lots of scary 'troll' voices and choose the best and most ferocious version!

▶ All the other lines can be chanted in unison (all together).

▶ Use different instruments in verses 4, 6 and 8 for the sound of the goats crossing the bridge. Try quiet pairs of pencils (verse 4), louder claves or woodblocks (verse 6), and tambourines and drums (verse 8).

Little Red Riding Hood

Looking so cool
Wearing a red hoodie,
But this little girl
Is definitely a goodie!

Did some baking,
Cupcakes she made.
Off to see Grandma
To make a trade.

Walking fast,
Hearing a sound.
Keep to the path,
Don't look around!

Arrives at Grandma's,
Opens the door,
Sees dirty footprints,
All over the floor!

'Grandma, Grandma,
Your eyes look huge,
And your cheeks are hairy,
Or is that rouge?'

The wolf blinked his eyes
And gave a big smile.
'So I can see you,
My sweet chile!'

'Grandma, Grandma,
Your ears stand so tall,
And your finger nails
Need a cut, that's all.'

The wolf wiggled his ears
And gave a bigger smile.
'So I can hear you,
My sweet chile!'

'Grandma, Grandma,
Your teeth are so big!
And is that your hair
Or are you wearing a wig?'

The wolf twitched his nose
And opened his jaws
And gobbled up Red
And her hoodie of course.

Then came a hunter
Armed with a knife,
And cut down the wolf
To save the girl's life.

Out jumped Grandma
And little Red too.
Now don't talk to strangers,
Whatever you do!

Performance extras

▶ Read through the complete rap and talk about different characters.

▶ Add taps, claps or stamps to the beat of the rap.

▶ Chant all narrative verses in unison (all together), or choose confident children to try solo verses.

▶ Cast a soloist for the part of Little Red Riding Hood.

▶ Experiment with scary wolf voices and choose a good one for the wolf solo part.

▶ Say the last two lines of the rap much louder as a 'warning'!

▶ In verse 3, vary the tempo (fast and slow) and explore some possible spooky sound effects.

▶ Choose a simple rhythm pattern to be tapped on drums or claves in between each verse. Ask children to get louder very gradually to increase the tension.

▶ Act out the drama as the rap is performed.

Goldilocks

Three bears in their pad,
Baby bear, mum and dad,
One small, one not so small
And one huge, I might add!

Mother bear makes some food
But nobody is in the mood;
So off they go for a walk,
And they don't hear Goldie's knock.

In she goes and sees the bowls
Of porridge on the table;
She smiles and takes a taste from each,
As fast as she is able.

Three bowls made for bears,
Baby bear, mum and dad,
One small, one not so small
And one huge, I might add!

Then she turns and sees the chairs
For three bears by the table;
She smiles and takes a turn in each,
As fast as she is able.

Three chairs made for bears
Baby bear, mum and dad,
One small, one not so small
And one huge, I might add!

Now she climbs up the stairs,
Finds the beds beneath the gable;
She smiles and takes a turn in each,
As fast as she is able.

Three beds made for bears,
Baby bear, mum and dad,
One small, one not so small
And one huge, I might add!

She falls asleep in baby's bed,
All cosy, small and neat;
But when the three bears do return,
All three she'll have to meet!

Three bears with hungry tums,
Baby bear, mum and dad,
One small, one not so small
And one huge, I might add!

Three bears returning now,
Standing still, looking round;
One empty bowl they spy,
And now look what they found.

Saw Baby's chair, all in bits,
Nowhere for him to sit!
Tears rolling down his face –
Who has done this to their place?

Upstairs, go those three bears;
Baby bear, mum and dad.
And Baby's bed is full as well –
Who's this girl? Who can tell?

Up she wakes, and looks around,
And sees furry faces three.
She squeals and looks again:
'Three teddy bears for me!'

Performance extras

► Read through the complete rap and talk about different characters.

► Add taps, claps or stamps to the beat of the rap.

► Try using a soloist for the purple verses. All the others can be chanted in unison.

► Choose three contrasting sounds for the repeated lines:

One small, one not so small

And one huge, I might add!

► Play a quiet sound on the first 'small', a louder sound on the second 'small', and a loud sound on 'huge'.

► Add a solo girl voice for Goldie's squeal and last line!

► Provide bear masks and choose three children to act out the roles of the three bears using props.

► This is not the expected ending. Do the children like it? Write an alternative scary ending where Goldilocks runs away!

Noah's Ark

"There's going to be a flood!
We must get out the 'hood,"
Said Noah.

"The Lord says it will rain,
Again and again!"
Said Noah.

"Let's build a boat,
And make sure it will float,"
Said Noah.

"Chop and cut the wood,
Make it strong and good",
Said Noah.

"Fill it with animals,
Birds and bees and mammals,"
Said Noah.

"Elephants and cats,
And crocodiles and rats!"
Said Noah.

"Two of every kind —
Nobody will mind,"
Said Noah.

So that's what they have done,
And "The rain it has begun!"
Said Noah.

The rain poured down
"But nobody will drown,"
Said Noah.

"It rained for forty years,
And then the skies did clear,"
Said Noah.

"I'll send out a raven
To try and find a haven,"
Said Noah.

The bird came back,
"His feathers were black,"
Said Noah.

So off flew a dove,
"The bird of love,"
Said Noah.

"The ark came to stop
Upon a mountain top,"
Said Noah.

"It's safe to go home,
No need to roam,"
Said Noah.

"There'll be no more rain
Or flooding again!"
Said Noah.

"The rainbow in the sky
Is a promise from up high."
Said Noah.

Performance extras

▶ Read through the complete rap and talk about different characters.

▶ Add taps, claps or stamps to the beat of the rap.

▶ Treat 'Said Noah' as a choral refrain chanted by all the children. Try clapping three times in between each verse.

▶ Use one or multiple soloists for different verses.

▶ Add boat-building sound effects to verses 3 and 4 using wooden instruments such as claves, woodblocks, guiros, etc.

▶ Add animal sound effects to verses 5 - 7 using voices.

▶ Add rain sound effects to verses 8 - 10 using rainsticks, maracas, glockenspiels, etc.

▶ Use animal masks and act out the animals filling and leaving the ark.

▶ Can children think of any other animals to include in some brand new verses of their own? Include them after verse 6.

The Gingerbread Man

"I'm going to bake, and I'm going to make
A treat to eat for tea.
A gingerbread man, so fat and sweet
That's what I'll make – you'll see!"

The baker mixed and he rolled and he baked
The finest biscuits ever made;
And as the oven door was opened,
There he heard the biscuit say:

"Don't you eat me! You won't eat me!
Just you wait and see!
Run, run as fast as you can,
You can't catch me – I'm the gingerbread man!"

Across the floor and out the door
Ran the finest gingerbread man,
Followed then by baker and wife –
As fast as they could, they ran!

He passed a pig, wearing a wig
Who fancied a little treat.
"Stop", the pig cried, "and wait awhile,
For you I'm keen to eat!"

"Don't you eat me! You won't eat me!
Just you wait and see!
Run, run as fast as you can,
You can't catch me – I'm the gingerbread man!"

He passed a cow, taking a bow
Who fancied a little treat.
"Stop", she cried, "and wait awhile,
For you I'm keen to eat!"

"Don't you eat me! You won't eat me!
Just you wait and see!
Run, run as fast as you can,
You can't catch me – I'm the gingerbread man!"

He passed a horse (staring, of course),
Who fancied a little treat.
"Stop", she cried, "and wait awhile,
For you I'm keen to eat!"

"Don't you eat me! You won't eat me!
Just you wait and see!
Run, run as fast as you can,
You can't catch me – I'm the gingerbread man!"

He passed a dog, sitting on a log,
Who fancied a little treat.
"Stop", she cried, "and wait awhile,
For you I'm keen to eat!"

"Don't you eat me! You won't eat me!
Just you wait and see!
Run, run as fast as you can,
You can't catch me – I'm the gingerbread man!"

He came to a river and began to shiver,
As he heard sounds behind him.
"Now I'm stuck, they're going to catch me –
And I don't know how to swim!"

A sly old fox, sitting by some rocks
At the flowing water's edge.
"I will help you. Jump on my back.
To this I give my pledge!"

The fox did float and to his coat
The gingerbread man held tight.
But halfway across the fox turned around
And gave him such a fright!

Fox gave a grin and pointed at his chin,
"Move yourself up here."
The gingerbread man, he climbed along...
And then did disappear!

Now fox did smile, and in a while
He climbed out on the shore.

Poor gingerbread man, sweet biscuit man,
Never to be seen no more.

Performance extras

▶ Read through the rap and ask children to listen out for repeated lines. All the lines not spoken by a character can be chanted in unison.

▶ Choose a confident child to read the gingerbread man chants. Try using a sing-song voice for the "Run, run, as fast as you can" parts, as though taunting the other characters.

▶ Invite children to try the different animal characters – pig, cow, horse and dog. Provide masks. Can they act out the actions too?

▶ Add appropriate vocal animal sound effects as the gingerbread man escapes each animal.

▶ The fox needs to be a very persuasive character, with a voice to match!

▶ Add watery sound effects for the last five verses using maracas, rainsticks and glockenspiels.

▶ Have fun acting out the drama with all the characters chasing the gingerbread man to the water's edge, and then watching him come to a sticky end!

Three Little Pigs

Three little pigs,
Thrown out of their digs,
Looking for somewhere new.
"Let's find some stuff
And build something tough –
Yes, that's just what we'll do!"

The first little pig
Found some straw,
And built up a house quite small.
Along came the wolf,
Whose name was Rolf,
And looked at it over the wall.

He called to the pig
Who danced a jig
And didn't care at all.
"I'll huff and I'll puff
And I'll flatten your house!"
And down the house did fall!

The second little pig
Found some twigs,
And built up a house so tall.
Along came the wolf,
Whose name was Rolf,
And looked at it over the wall.

He called to the pigs
Who danced two jigs
And didn't care at all.
"I'll huff and I'll puff
And I'll flatten your house!"
And down the house did fall!

The third little pig
Found some bricks,
And built a house so strong.
Along came the wolf,
Whose name was Rolf,
And looked at it hard and long.

He called to the pigs
Who danced three jigs
And didn't care at all.
"I'll huff and I'll puff
And I'll flatten your house!" –

But that didn't happen at all!
The wolf thought hard,
And still kept guard,
And then he had a thought.
I'll try again!" And so he did,
But still it came to nought.

The pigs inside
Laughed til they cried
At the efforts the wolf had made.
And so the wolf
Climbed on the roof
And the pigs inside just played.

The fire was hot,
They boiled the pot,
And stirred the soup around.
The wolf fell down
And burned his nose,
And slid right to the ground!

He howled and howled
And then he growled,
And ran right out the door.
The pigs waved bye
And chased him off,
And Rolf was seen no more!

Performance extras

▶ Read through the complete rap and talk about different characters.

▶ Add taps, claps or stamps to the beat of the rap.

▶ This can all be rapped in unison (all together) except for the last line of verse 1 and a few choice lines from Rolf the wolf.

▶ The three little pigs can act out building their houses, accompanied by suitable sound effects: for verse 2, try using plastic straws or pencils tapped quietly together; for verse 4, use pairs of claves tapped together; and for verse 6, pairs of wooden bricks or castanets tapped together loudly.

▶ Encourage the three little pigs to dance jigs as the rap is performed.

▶ For verses 3 and 5, add a noisy sound effect for the houses falling down.

▶ Act out the drama using masks and props.

Snow White

My hair is black as coal
My skin is white as snow
So can you guess my name?
That's what I'd like to know.

Mirror, mirror, on the wall,
Who's the fairest of them all?

My stepmother the Queen is cruel,
As you will see.
She hates me for my beauty –
She's got it in for me!

Mirror, mirror on the wall,
Who's the fairest of them all?

When the mirror names me
She swears this cannot be.
I've had to run away
So I can still be free!

Mirror, mirror, on the wall,
Who's the fairest of them all?

Then I met seven little men
Who want to care for me.
Seven little hats worn on their heads; I
clean and cook their tea.

Happy, Sleepy, Sneezy, Grumpy,
Dopey, Bashful, Doc,
Seven dwarves with seven names,
Mining in the rock.

Mirror, mirror, on the wall,
Who's the fairest of them all?

They nod and smile and say to me
"We'll see you in the morning!"
The seven dwarves with seven hats,
Give Snow White this warning:

"Don't you open up that door,
Don't speak to a stranger.
We will try to protect you,
To keep you from danger."

Mirror, mirror, on the wall,
Who's the fairest of them all?

I hear a knock upon the door
Open it wide to see,
An old lady with an apple red,
She gives the apple to me.

The fruit looks sweet and very juicy
So I take a bite,
But then my knees, they do give way
And I fall without a fight!

Mirror, mirror, on the wall,
Who's the fairest of them all?

Seven dwarves with seven beards,
Come and find me sleeping,
Place me in a clear glass tomb,
All the while a-weeping.

Years later comes a prince who sees
Me in this state of peace;
He frees me with a kiss of love,
And all my troubles cease.

Mirror, mirror, on the wall,
Who's the fairest of them all?

"Snow White!"

Performance extras

▶ Read through the complete rap and talk about the different characters.

▶ Add taps, claps or stamps to the beat of the rap.

▶ This rap is written in the first person, so choose a confident child to read the main part. Alternatively, chant it in unison and invite children to mime actions to the words.

▶ The chorus in purple can be chanted by everyone in unison, or sung to the tune of 'Rain, rain, go away'.

▶ Add a magical sound effect before each repetition of the 'mirror' chorus.

▶ Choose seven children to act out the characters of the seven dwarves.

Hansel and Gretel

Hansel and Gretel, hand in hand,
Walking through the wooded land.
Dropping pebbles as they go
So the way home they will know.

Hansel and Gretel, arm in arm,
Drop crumbs to keep from harm.
Birds swoop down and eat the bread
And the children, they get lost instead!

Hansel and Gretel, side by side,
Try to find somewhere to hide.
Wander round and round the trees
A house of candy they do see!

A little house built all from cakes,
Biscuits, bread and other bakes.
Windows clear with sugar fine,
And of the owner, there's no sign.

Hansel and Gretel, cheek by cheek,
Eat enough sweets to last a week,
Until they hear a voice so sweet –
Someone surely safe to meet?

Hansel and Gretel, hand in hand,
In the witch's house they stand.
She locked poor Hansel in a cage
And looked at Gretel in a rage.

"I want this boy all fattened up,
So I can eat him for my sup,
And you, my girl, will cook for him.
Make sure that he's not too thin!"

Hansel and Gretel, day by day,
Made a plan to make her pay.
When she came to look at him
Hansel stuck out a bone so thin.

"Why is he not getting fatter?
I want to serve him on a platter.
Make some food and make it rich.
Cook up such a fancy dish!"

Hansel and Gretel make a plan,
Gretel cooks a delicious flan.
Calls the witch to come and taste,
And down she trips in her haste.

Hansel and Gretel, minute by minute,
Heat the oven and push her in it!
Now they're free to run away,
Back home they can go to stay.

Performance extras

▶ Read through the complete rap and talk about the different characters.

▶ Add taps, claps or stamps to the beat of the rap.

▶ This can all be performed in unison (all together). Alternatively, choose two children to say 'Hansel and Gretel' together each time it occurs at the start of a verse.

▶ Ask for a volunteer to read the witch's words in a suitably scary voice!

▶ Invent a simple rhythm pattern to tap, clap or play in between each verse. Can the children vary the dynamics (loud and quiet) to increase the tension as the rap progresses?

▶ Have fun making a collage house out of sweet wrappers, as a backdrop.

Musicians of Bremen

[Donkey]
There's no place for me here!
I shall run right away,
And find a band I can join
This very same day.

A musician am I;
The lute is my sound.
To Bremen I'll go –
The best place around.

[He meets an old dog]
There's no place for you here!
Let's run right away;
You can join my band
This very same day.

[Dog]
A musician am I;
The drums are my sound.
To Bremen I'll go –
The best place around.

[He meets an old cat]
There's no place for you here!
Let's run right away;
You can join my band
This very same day.

[Cat]
A musician am I;
Singing is my sound.
To Bremen I'll go –
The best place around.

[He meets a rooster]
There's no place for you here!
Let's run right away;
You can join my band
This very same day.

[Rooster]
A musician am I;
Crowing is my sound.
To Bremen I'll go –
The best place around.

The donkey's back was broad and strong
So on it, dog stood tall and bold.
The cat sat next and on the top
Perched rooster, so it's told.

Rooster flew to the top of a tree,
A house he saw with a light shining clear;
And a table laid with things to eat,
And a band of robbers full of cheer.

"We could do with some of their feast!"
And so they came up with a plot.
The rooster crowed, the cat meowed,
Dog barked and donkey brayed – a lot.

Musicians are we;
Noise is our sound!
To Bremen we'll go –
The best place around!

The robbers leapt up
All seeing a ghost,
And rushed from the house
Fearing the worst!

Soon after midnight,
the robbers crept back.
Saw cat's eyes glowing like hot coals;
Dog bites, donkey kicks, rooster crows –
A witch had come to claim their souls!

The robbers ran in fear, and trembling;
The noise had scared them to their boots!
And four new friends sat round the table,
Singing songs and musical notes.

Musicians are we;
Noise is our sound.
To Bremen we'll go
The best place around!

Performance extras

► Read through the complete rap and talk about the different characters.
► Add taps, claps or stamps to the beat of the rap.
► Choose four children to play the parts of the donkey, dog, cat and rooster.
► Each character needs a different instrument sound, for instance: guitar (elastic bands stretched over an empty tissue box), drum, voice and guiro (scraper).
► In verse 11 the characters can use instruments or voices to add sound effects for the 'music'.
► Have fun acting out the story as the rap is performed.

Sol-fa singing rap

Open your trap, try a singing rap,
Sing these words and rhymes.
Lick your lips and wiggle your tongue
And sing these lots of times.

Soh me, soh me, soh me doh,
Soh me, soh me, ray.
Soh me, soh me, soh me doh,
Sing throughout the day.

Starting now, try a singing rap,
Sounds both high and low.
Stretch your mouth and grit your teeth
And sing this fast and slow.

Soh me, soh me, soh me doh,
Soh me, soh me, ray.
Soh me, soh me, soh me doh,
Sing throughout the day.

Now breathe in, and then breathe out,
Stand up tall and strong.
Hold your head up high and smile,
Sing sounds short and long.

Soh me, soh me, soh me doh,
Soh me, soh me, ray.
Soh me, soh me, soh me doh,
Sing throughout the day.

Performance extras

▶ Before trying this rap, practise some echo singing using 'soh me' (the 'cuckoo' notes) – or use G and E chime bars for these notes. Use hand signs (see Resources, page 88) and ask children to copy or echo what you sing and do.

▶ Ask children to contrast between a 'rapping' style for the verses and using a singing voice for the chorus.

▶ Add taps, claps or stamps to the beat of the rap. Alternatively, add the 'soh me' notes using chime bars, hand chimes or boomwhackers.

▶ Listen to 'Doe, a deer' from 'The Sound of Music' to hear all the sol-fa notes.

Nursery rhyme gang

Humpty Dumpty sat on the hill
Waiting to meet Jack and Jill.
Up came the Grand Old Duke of York
Wanting to have a little talk.

We're in the nursery rhyme gang!
Along came Little Miss Muffet and Polly
Searching for spiders and a very sick dolly;
And Jack Horner followed with Little Bo-Peep
Trying to find one special black sheep.
We're in the nursery rhyme gang!

Simple Simon brought some pies
And Georgie Porgie came in disguise.
The mouse ran up the clock to see
Mary Mary come over the lea.
We're in the nursery rhyme gang!

The Queen of Hearts met old Mother Hubbard
Who brought along her famous cupboard.
And Ole King Cole was almost late
As twenty-four blackbirds flew by the gate.
We're in the nursery rhyme gang!

The stars came out and twinkled on high,
A cow was seen jumping in the sky.
The blind mice found their way through the park
And all together they met in the dark.
We're in the nursery rhyme gang!

Performance extras

▶ Read through the complete rap and talk about different characters.

▶ Add taps, claps or stamps to the beat of the rap.

▶ Children can learn two line couplets or complete verses to rap.

▶ Try rapping the last line of each verse in unison.

▶ Add a drum beat to the rap playing on the beat throughout.

▶ Hold up pictures of the different nursery rhymes at suitable places in the performance.

▶ Have fun dressing up as the different nursery rhyme characters.

▶ How many different nursery rhymes can the children identify from the rap? Learn some of the less well-known original rhymes.

▶ Relate to early years topics e.g. 'Nursery rhymes', 'Stories' and 'Friends'.

Summer holiday

We're all going on a summer holiday!
Just a few days away,
In summer we can go,
Whatever the weather,
Come rain or snow.

We're all going on a summer holiday!
The sky is blue,
The day is fine.
On this summer holiday
The sun will shine.

We're all going on a summer holiday!
Pack our bags,
With clothes and shoes.
Take some toys,
Which shall I choose?

We're all going on a summer holiday!
Drinks and games,
To play in the car.
Hope the journey's
Not too far!

We're all going on a summer holiday!
A penny for the first
To see the sea.
I just know
That's going to be me!

We're all going on a summer holiday!
Mum is driving,
Dad's asleep.
You and me,
We're counting sheep.

At the beach, we can build castles
In the sand, on the land, with our hands.
At the beach, we can eat ice creams,
Vanilla, choc, peppermint rock.
At the beach, we can play cricket,
Football, catch, volleyball match.
At the beach, we can go paddling,
Swim, splash, rockpool dash.

We're all going on a summer holiday!
The day is done,
It's time to go.
Homeward bound,
End of the show!

Performance extras

▶ Read through the complete rap and talk about different verses.

▶ Add taps, claps or stamps to the beat of the rap.

▶ Try singing together the purple first line to the tune of famous song 'We're all going on a summer holiday'.

▶ Choose soloists to rap the different verses.

▶ The eight-line break can be chanted all together or rapped by a confident soloist.

▶ Use this rap in early years topics such as 'Summer', 'Holidays', 'Journeys', etc.

Starlight rap

Twinkle, twinkle, little star,
Stay alight, shining far.
In the dark sky, burning bright,
That's the sign of a starlit night.

Twinkle, twinkle, little bat,
Flying blind, no time to chat.
In the dark sky, soaring sprite,
That's the sign of a starlit night.

Twinkle, twinkle, crescent moon,
We can see you shining soon.
In the dark sky, such a sight,
That's the sign of a starlit night.

Twinkle, twinkle, little owl,
Hunting high and low, you prowl.
In the dark sky, caught in flight,
That's the sign of a starlit night.

Twinkle, twinkle, fiery comet,
Zooming past just like a rocket.
In the dark sky, quite a height,
That's the sign of a starlit night.

Twinkle, twinkle, clever fox,
Hiding down behind the rocks.
In the dark sky, ready to fight,
That's the sign of a starlit night.

Twinkle, twinkle, shooting star,
Falling fast, where you are.
In the dark sky, sparkling light,
That's the sign of a starlit night.

Twinkle, twinkle, lost in space,
Planets in solar system race.
In the dark sky, sparkling light,
That's the sign of a starlit night.

Performance extras

▶ Read through the complete rap and talk about different subjects in the verses.

▶ Add taps, claps or stamps to the beat of the rap.

▶ Treat the lines in purple as a chorus and use unison voices.

▶ Use soloists for each verse.

▶ Choose different metal instruments to create 'twinkling' sounds, such as triangles, Indian bells, jingle bells, chime bars, glockenspiels, etc.

▶ Relate to early years topics such as 'Day and night', 'Animals', 'Space', etc.

Counting body beat rap

I can keep the beat with my feet,
With my hands, with my seat,
Nod my head, count instead:
1, 2, 3, 4, 5, 6, 7, 8.

I can keep the beat with my toes,
With my fingers, with my nose,
Tap my knees, give a squeeze,
1, 2, 3, 4, 5, 6, 7, 8.

I can keep the beat with my heart,
With my eyes, make a start,
Bend my back, jumping jack,
1, 2, 3, 4, 5, 6, 7, 8.

I can keep the beat with my head,
With my legs, then play dead,
Curl up small, stand up tall,
1 2 3 4 5, 6 7, 8.

I can keep the beat with my bones,
With some skin, with some stones,
Tap some bricks, pairs of sticks,
1, 2, 3, 4, 5, 6 7, 8.

I can keep the beat with a mix,
With some kicks, with some clicks,
Try some claps, and some taps,
1, 2, 3, 4, 5, 6, 7, 8!
I can keep the beat with my bones,
With some skin, with some stones,
Tap some bricks, pairs of sticks,
1, 2, 3, 4, 5, 6 7, 8.

I can keep the beat with a mix,
With some kicks, with some clicks,
Try some claps, and some taps,
1, 2, 3, 4, 5, 6, 7, 8!

Performance extras

► Read through the complete rap and talk about different actions.

► Try out the actions for each verse.

► Add a regular drum beat to the beat of the rap.

► Invite all the children to chant together the numbers in the last line of each verse. Can they count on their fingers as they chant?

► Can they think of different ways of chanting the numbers? For instance, vary the dynamics (loud/quiet), start quietly and get louder, use different voices, etc.

► Use with early years topics such as 'All about me', 'The body', 'Numbers', etc.

Shoe shuffle rap

These shoes are made for walking,
These shoes are made for running,
These shoes are made for jumping,
What will your shoes choose to do?

Flat shoes, high shoes, wellington boots,
Pumps and trainers, which will suit?
Sandals, flip-flops, show your toes,
Smart shoes, new shoes, anything goes!

These shoes are made for skating,
These shoes are made for dancing,
These shoes are made for kicking,
What will your shoes choose to do?

Shiny shoes, best shoes, quite a hit,
Old shoes, shabby shoes, which still fit,
Dancing slippers and football boots,
Shoes to show your favourite roots.

These shoes are made for marching,
These shoes are made for hopping,
These shoes are made for skipping,
What will your shoes choose to do?

Lost shoes, found shoes, odd ones out,
Clogs and sneakers, without a doubt,
All are worn to keep our feet,
Shuffling and moving down the street.

Performance extras

► Read through the complete rap and talk about different shoes and moves.
► Add taps, claps or stamps to the beat of the rap.
► Vary the two styles in this rap.
► Say the purple verses in a more 'sung' style. Add appropriate actions.
► Try rapping the other verses in a contrasting style.
► Use this rap with early years topics e.g. 'Clothes', 'Shopping' and 'Movement'.

The food wrap rap

Sandwiches, sandwiches,
Clap, clap, clap!
All my favourites
In the food wrap rap.

Take a tasty filling, wrap it in some bread –
You've got a sandwich to eat instead!

Sandwiches, sandwiches,
Clap, clap, clap!
All my favourites
In the food wrap rap.
Chicken mayonnaise, chocolate spread & jam,
Tuna-fish and thick pink ham!

Sandwiches, sandwiches,
Clap, clap, clap!
All my favourites
In the food wrap rap.

Slices of salami, chunks of cheese,
Add some healthy salad, yesssss please!

Sandwiches, sandwiches,
Clap, clap, clap!
All my favourites
In the food wrap rap.

Bacon and tomato, honey and grapes,
Cut the bread into interesting shapes.

Sandwiches, sandwiches,
Clap, clap, clap!
All my favourites
In the food wrap rap.

White bread, brown bread, crispy rolls,
Try granary, seeded and bread with holes.

Sandwiches, sandwiches,
Clap, clap, clap!
All my favourites
In the food wrap rap.

Soft baguettes and pitta breads,
Fill them all with your choice of spreads.

Sandwiches, sandwiches,
Clap, clap, clap!
All my favourites
In the food wrap rap.

Performance extras

▶ Read through the complete rap and talk about different subjects in the verses.

▶ Add taps, claps or stamps to the beat of the rap.

▶ Chant the repeated chorus in unison and add claps.

▶ Choose soloists to rap the different verses in between.

▶ Try making some of these sandwich varieties with the children. Which are their favourite fillings? Can they think of some other fillings and write some new verses?

▶ Use this rap with early years topics such as 'All about me', 'Food', 'Healthy eating', etc.

Christmas wrapping

Time to do some Christmas prep,
Take it carefully, step by step.
My hands are clapping and my feet go tap,
This is the Christmas wrapping rap!

Wrapping paper for wrapping gifts,
Wrapping should be done in shifts!
My hands are clapping and my feet go tap,
This is the Christmas wrapping rap!

Christmas trees are wrapped in glitter,
The wind is blowing, cold and bitter.
My hands are clapping and my feet go tap,
This is the Christmas wrapping rap!

Coloured lights blink on and off,
Most of us have a cold or a cough.
My hands are clapping and my feet go tap,
This is the Christmas wrapping rap!

Wrap up warm, keep out the cold,
Presents bought and presents sold.
My hands are clapping and my feet go tap,
This is the Christmas wrapping rap!

Singing carols in a show,
Go to parties and play in the snow.
My hands are clapping and my feet go tap,
This is the Christmas wrapping rap.

The story of Jesus is told once again,
With donkeys and shepherds and three wise men.
My hands are clapping and my feet go tap,
This is the Christmas wrapping rap!

Travelling to see a new baby King,
Surrounded by angels waiting to sing.
My hands are clapping and my feet go tap,
This is the Christmas wrapping rap!

And Christmas Eve comes at last,
With all the memories of Christmas past.
My hands are clapping and my feet go tap,
This is the Christmas wrapping rap!

Who's that wrapped in a warm red suit,
With a long white beard and shiny black boots?
My hands are clapping and my feet go tap,
This is the Christmas wrapping rap!

Laughs like this: 'Ho, ho, ho!' –
Santa Claus in the snow, snow, snow.
My hands are clapping and my feet go tap,
This is the Christmas wrapping rap!

Performance extras

▶ Read through the complete rap and talk about different characters.

▶ Try taps, claps or stamps to the beat of the rap.

▶ Treat the repeated lines as a unison chorus, chanted by all the children together.

▶ Add actions such as claps and taps to the repeated chorus.

▶ Choose soloists to learn and chant different verses.

▶ Let children dress up as nativity characters or Santa with his sleigh full of presents, and create a tableau.

▶ Add Christmas sound effects such as jingle bells, tambourines, and triangles to appropriate verses.

Listening list

Classical music with a strong beat:

▶ Carl Orff: Carmina Burana (O Fortuna)

▶ Gustav Holst: The Planets Suite (Mars)

▶ Wolfgang Amadeus Mozart: Turkish March

▶ Johann Strauss: Radetzky March

▶ Paul Dukas: The Sorcerer's Apprentice

▶ John Philip Souza: The Liberty Bell

▶ Other military marches

Music that changes tempo (fast/slow):

▶ Georges Bizet: L'Arlésienne (Farandole)

▶ Edvard Grieg: Peer Gynt Suite (In the Hall of the Mountain King)

▶ Arthur Honegger: Pacific 231

▶ Heitor Villa-Lobos: The Little Train of Caipira

▶ Taraf de Haidouks: Gypsy music

Pop/rock music with a strong beat:

Most pop and rock songs have a good, strong beat. Good examples are:

▶ Queen: We will rock you

▶ Robbie Williams: Angels

▶ The Beatles: Get Back

▶ The White Stripes: Seven Nation Army

▶ Black Eyed Peas: Where is the love?

▶ Outkast: Hey Ya

▶ Most dance music

Music with repeated patterns (Ostinato/riffs):

▶ Maurice Ravel: Boléro

▶ Ludwig van Beethoven: Symphony no. 7 - Allegretto (2nd movement)

▶ Johann Pachelbel: Canon in D Major

- Igor Stravinksy: The Rite of Spring (Introduction)
- Steve Reich: Music for 18 Musicians
- The Beatles: Day Tripper
- Deep Purple: Smoke on the Water
- Dave Brubeck: Take Five
- Stevie Wonder: Superstition

Resources

Meet Sam and Susie

These rhythm symbols can be photocopied and laminated to create notation cards for 'Sam' and 'Susie'.

Sol-fa hand signs

Use these hand signs in the Sol-fa singing rap (see page 74).

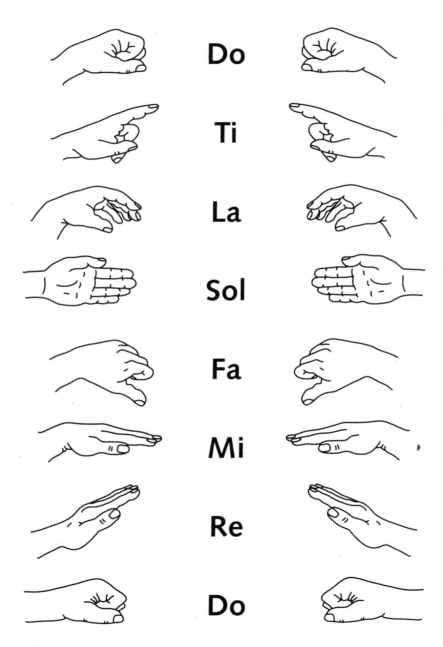

Do

Ti

La

Sol

Fa

Mi

Re

Do